A DAY AT THE PARK

Fiction for Seniors

seniorality

chapter 1
The Call

THE ALARM CLOCK went off at six o'clock in the morning, just as it always did. My daughter keeps asking me why I set it, now that I am retired from my job, but I feel comforted by the routine. I also like to sit and have my coffee – two milks, no sugar and watch the sunrise.

My twelve-year-old cat jumps up on the bed to gently nuzzle and bump my face. His whiskers twitch and tickle my cheek.

"Good morning, Sam", I say aloud and shoo him off the bed. He jumps off as I throw back the covers.

As I walk down the hallway, I am lost in thought about what I will do with myself today. Last night, the weatherman on the news said that it would be a warm, sunny weekend. I was so happy because it felt like I had been in this house for too long!

The rich smell of coffee fills my nose as I walk through the kitchen door. The strong smell is one I have always loved. Thank goodness for automatic coffee makers!

I open a can of shrimp flavored cat food for Sam and pour it carefully on a dish. He pushes his nose in my way the entire time. I am always amazed at how hungry he seems.

As I pet his soft, gray head, the calendar on the wall catches my eye. A big pink circle surrounds today's date and I step closer to see what I marked.

The smile on my face grows as I realize why I thought today was so important. It's the first day of spring. The saying about the month of March coming in like a lion and out like a lamb was true where I live. Spring can either be very cold or very hot. In the same week, it can be both!

I was happy to see through my kitchen window that on this day the sunshine would be bright and warm. The weatherman's predictions should be right and I am going to have a fine day.

A loud, long beep stops my thoughts. My coffee is ready. I pour the hot liquid into my favorite mug. It is an oversized, cream-colored mug that says "The World's Best Nana". My granddaughter gave it to me last Christmas and I love it. My granddaughter Ella means the world to me.

I blow the steam across my coffee mug. I think for a moment about Ella. Her big brown eyes and sweet smile with some missing milk teeth always bring me joy. She looks just like her mother did at that age.

The phone rings and once again my thoughts are interrupted. I walk over to the phone cradle, stepping carefully around my cat, Sam. He is weaving his thin body in and out of my legs. I suppose he is saying thanks for breakfast.

"Hello?"

"Hi, Nana", says a little voice on the other end of the line.

"Oh, Ella! Hi, angel. How are you this morning?"

"Good. I am playing with my baby dolls."

"Oh that sounds fun. Guess what I'm going to do today?" I say and wait for her to respond.

"What?" she asks.

"I am going to the park. It is just too beautiful to stay inside. I would love for someone to come with me. Would you like to go with me?"

"Yay! Yes, Nana. I'll go with you. I'll walk over with Mama in a minute."

"Ok, El. I'll see you soon."

I press the "off" button with my thumb and place the phone on the counter.

I take a deep breath and smile again. It's going to be a good day. I can already tell. It is one thing to be outside in warmer weather, but it will be even better to be outside with my granddaughter.

I go back to the counter and take a sip of coffee. In my mind I go through my closet while I finish drinking my coffee. For the first day of spring, I am going to need a cheerful outfit for our day at the park.

chapter 2
The Gift

ALL OF THE clothes in my closet bring me joy. Some of them were cheerful indeed. I fan slowly through the clothes hanging in my closet and touch each blouse. It is so nice to have lovely things. I take down a lovely pink shirt and hold it up to myself as I look in the mirror.

"Perfect," I whisper.

I hurry through the rest of my morning routine. I brush my teeth, run a comb through my hair, and rub deodorant under my arms. My skin looks pale from winter, so I put on just enough makeup to brighten my face. I remind myself to put a camera in my tote bag before I leave. I want to make sure to capture some memories today for photographs later.

I walk back into the kitchen to gather the rest of the items I need for the day. I know Ella will want to feed the ducks and the turtles, so I take a half loaf of bread from the bread box. I squeeze it gently through the bag. It was perfect for day because it was starting to get stale. That will be perfect for the animals at the park.

I put the bread into my tote bag along with two bottles of water, my camera, a small picnic blanket, and a bag of cookies to share with Ella. I took a moment to think if I forgot anything.

Oh yes! I did forget something. Last week when I went to the mall, I bought Ella a gift. Today was a good day to give it to her. It is still lying in its box on my dresser.

I smile a little as I pick up her gift. She will love the box as much as the gift inside, I think. The box is hot pink with shimmery purple mermaid scales. Little girls like my Ella love these things.

Inside the box is a little silver bracelet. Three charms hang from it. The first charm is Ella's initial, a tiny "E" made out of tiny, shiny rhinestones on a silver disc. The second charm is a pink heart that is shiny and eye-catching. The third charm is a little mermaid with bright pink scales on her tail.

I can't wait to give the bracelet to her. I hope she will like it.

Just as I am walking back into the kitchen, I hear the door burst open and little feet come thumping into the room.

"NANA!"

Ella leaps toward me with so much energy and squeezes me around my middle with her chubby arms. I squeeze her back as I try not to fall over from the powerful hug. I smooth down her wild, curly hair and give my daughter-in-law a big smile.

"Hi, sweet girl! I'm so glad you're coming to the park with me today. We are going to have so much fun."

Ella is five years old. Like most children that age, she has a way of knowing when her Nana has bought her a gift. She sees the brightly colored box on the counter and looks at me with expectation on her face.

"Yes, that's yours. Go ahead and open it," I tell her.

She takes two skipping steps over to the counter and wastes no time ripping the lid off the box.

"Whoa", she says with a grin as she lifts the shiny bracelet from its tissue paper. "Will you hook it for me, Nana?"

I fumble just a bit as I hook the clasp for her. It is so tiny for anyone to get a hold of it. Once it is done, she shakes the charms around and makes them jingle. She hugs me again and thanks me for her gift.

My heart is so warm.

"Ok, are you ready? You look beautiful, I look beautiful. Let's go see what we can get into at the park!"

I check again to make sure I have everything we need. My daughter-in-law and I agree that I will walk Ella home after lunch. I add a light jacket to my tote bag just in case it is chilly in the shade. It always amazes me how it can be ten degrees cooler beneath a tree.

I close the door behind us, then I follow Ella's little bouncing body down the porch steps to the sidewalk. The park is only three blocks away. I already feel happiness warming my old bones. I turn my face up to the sun and take my granddaughter's hand.

chapter 3
Sights and Sound

WE LOVE the park near my house. It has fifteen acres of rolling green hills and flat ground that is perfect for a picnic. The black wrought iron gates has gorgeous scrollwork that greet visitors to the park. Ella stops and stands in front of the enormous gate and asks me to take her picture before we enter the park.

I dig into the bottom of my bag and finally come out with my camera. I snap a picture before Ella swings open the gate. The winding paths lead us beneath tall, grand weeping willows. The willow is my favorite kind of tree. I love to watch the long strands of leaves wave back and forth in the breeze. I stand for a moment and do just that.

"Those trees look like mermaid hair. It's long and green and it looks like it's waving under water", Ella says.

"I completely agree," I say.

Mermaid hair, I think to myself. That little girl has quite the imagination. As we continue our way down the path in the sunlight, I notice how wonderful the light wind feels as it lifts my hair from my neck. I take a deep breath and enjoy the sensation. It always feels good to shake off the cold of winter!

One of the main attractions of the park was on our right side. It is an oval-shaped lake with a fancy fountain in the center. There is plenty of seating around the lake, so Ella and I walk over and choose a bench right in front of the fountain.

We watch as the sprays of water burst into the air. They sparkle in the sunlight. Each stream of water would jump toward the sky in a pattern across the lake. After that, a beautiful arch of water stays in the air. In the sunlight it looks like a rainbow of diamonds. It is so lovely.

Ella is enchanted with the water show even though she has seen it many times before. To be honest, so am I. She leans against my side and rests her head on my shoulder as we enjoy the show.

Through the mist of the water spray, I can see the dog park on the other side of the fountain. Dogs of all shapes and sizes run and leap inside their fenced playground. A German Shepard and a spotted Dalmatian seem to be pulling on the same thing. I can't tell from this distance what the dogs are fighting over.

I bring my attention back to the fountain again. The pattern starts again. I can sense that Ella is ready to walk through the park and see what else we can find. She hops up from the bench and pulls on my hand.

"Let's keep walking," she suggests.

"Ok, let's go," I reply.

"Do you want to go watch the dogs for a few minutes?"

I see a flash of excitement in her eyes and she nods her head. This is a girl who loves dogs. Her parents keep telling her that she cannot have a dog of her own, but it doesn't stop Ella from trying. She asks at least once a week, I'm sure. She says she wants a Golden Retriever, but that she would settle for a bulldog. I hope one day her parents agree to get her a pet. It doesn't have to be a big dog because she will love it the same!

Hand in hand, we cross the wooden footbridge over the center of the lake. Ella poses for another picture like she is a superstar. We carefully lean as far out over the railing so we can get a closer look at all the turtles and fish swimming down below.

"We'll come back and feed them and the geese in a little bit, ok?"

Ella nods again as she watches a huge snapping turtle emerge from the water. It comes out of the water just enough to take a breath and blink his eyes slowly in the bright light. His sharp, pointed beak is a little scary. I make a note to keep our hands away from him when we come back to share our bread.

The entrance to the dog park is just to the right of the bridge. We open the seven-foot-high gate and walk into the observation area. Here we can watch the dogs' antics and games, but they will not bite or jump on us. Ella stands with her fingers laced between the chain links of the fence. She quietly watches the dogs play. The sounds of barking, panting, and owners calling to their pets fill the air around us.

I try to make a game of counting the dogs inside the park but they move too fast! I think I'll leave that game to Ella.

"Ready to go feed the geese?" I ask her. She jumped up and was ready to go.

chapter 4
Life Under Water

ELLA AND I decide to take the long way around to the lake. The path from the dog park continues through the trees.

Ella bends down to look at a pile of feathers on the ground beside the path.

"Look! What kind of bird did this come from?" she asks.

I take the biggest feather in my hand and run my fingers down its length. It is smooth and warm. It is black and gray and probably came from a pigeon. I tell Ella this and she looks a little disappointed.

"I thought it was from an owl," she frowns. "I like owls."

I ruffle her hair and place a kiss on her forehead. "Oh, I bet you're right. Now that I look at it closer, it does look like an owl feather."

We continue to make our way slowly back to the edge of the lake.

I place my bag on a bench and feel around inside for the old loaf of bread. My fingers finally find it and I pull it out of the tote bag.

We creep quietly closer to the water. We do not want to disturb the animals gathered there.

The surface of the water bubbles with fish popping up their heads in the hopes of catching a crumb. *They'll have to fight the geese and turtles*, I think to myself.

Ella opens the bread bag. I show her how to pull off small pieces and toss them far out into the lake. She does so.

All the geese begin to swim in that direction. They honk and bump into each other. Ella giggles as she watches them. A tiny turtle wanders into our area and Ella sits on the ground to hand feed it.

A big, fluffy cloud floats in front of the sun and puts us in the shade for the moment. I look up at the sky and see the most amazing sight.

Bright rays of sunlight stream from behind the cloud. Individual stripes of sunshine beam down to turn the lake into a beautiful, sparkling mirror. The sun's rays are so strong they look solid like you could touch them.

"Ella, look," I say, pointing to the sky.

She has always loved when the sun does that trick. She looks up for a second, gives me a thumbs up, and returns her attention to the turtle.

"Can I pick him up?" she asks.

"Sure, just be sure to wash your hands before we eat"

Ella reaches out to let the turtle walk onto her open hand. Suddenly she lets out a cry.

"Oh no! Where's my bracelet?" She holds up her arm to show me her bare wrist.

She stands up and begins to look all around. She puts her hands on her hips and looks deep in thought.

"We can retrace our steps before we leave and I bet we'll find it. Maybe it fell off while we were at the dog park."

We both look carefully through the grass and walk a little way down the path, but neither of us finds a mermaid bracelet.

Ella's shoulders slump as she plops onto the bench.

A man walks by on the path and waves to us. "Hello, how are you?" he calls out.

"We've been better," I say, "My granddaughter has lost her new bracelet." Ella gives him a half-hearted wave.

"Oh no. That's no good. I'll keep my eyes open for bracelets while I walk, ok?"

"You're very kind. It is a silver bracelet with mermaid and seashell charms on it."

The man tips his hat, an old worn-out baseball cap. He says, "Got it. Mermaids and seashells. Sounds like something my own granddaughter would like."

"Girls do go for that sort of thing, don't they?"

The man smiles and I notice how his eyes crinkle in the corners and how he has a dimple in his right cheek. He walks on saying to himself, "Mermaids and seashells..."

chapter 5
Lost and Found

ELLA AND I find a spot half in sun and half in shade. We decide that our stomachs need some real food.

After we spread the blue-striped blanket on the grass, I take out the grapes, carrots, tomatoes and strawberries along with cheese and crackers. Ella spends a lot of time building tall cheese towers between her crackers and then biting them while crumbs fall like rain from her mouth.

"Uh-oh. I'm making a huge mess," she says.

"No problem at all, sweet girl. We'll just shake the blanket off before we pack it up. Leave some food for the ants and birds, I guess."

She nods and goes on eating. I pop a few grapes in my mouth and nibble on a slice of cheese.

I watch a chipmunk wiggle his little white tail before darting up a tree beside us. A shimmering green dragonfly buzzes around us. His clear wings shine in the sun.

Ella jumps almost into my lap. She is afraid of bugs. I tell her, "Dragonflies do not bite or sting. All they do is fly around and look beautiful." She does not trust this information and sticks close by my side until the bug flies away.

Once our stomachs are full, we lie on our backs and watch the clouds float by above our heads.

We play the old game where each person has to tell what shape they see in a cloud and see if the other person can find it.

Ella's shapes are almost always animals. Sometimes she spots food in the clouds but usually it is lions, or unicorns, or puppies. The things I see are random. A castle. A shoe. A teapot. Ella always says she sees them.

There is a softball field not far from where we lay on our blanket gazing at the sky. The sounds of a friendly game drift over to us.

The tink sound of an aluminum bat hitting a ball is mixed with the chirp of birds overhead. All of these sounds give me the most peaceful feeling. It has been such a nice day already.

I hear the men's voices echo out across the field. They laugh and tease each other about their athletic skills.

I prop up on one elbow, so I can see the game. There is a loud thunk and the man at home base takes off, rounding the bases at full speed. I watch the ball as it flies high in the air. Two men chase the ball as it hits the ground and rolls to touch the outer fence of the field.

The man who hit the ball is almost back to home base by the time one man throws the ball.

"Home run," I say to myself. Ella is not paying attention to the softball game. She is looking at the giant playground across the path. Children swing and slide and jump. There are so many things to do on that playground.

"Do you want to go over there and play? We will be going home soon, dear."

"Yea, I want to swing," Ella replies. She stands up and a pile of cracker crumbs shower down onto the blanket. Both of us laugh.

"I'm leaving a lot of food for the ants," Ella says. She brushes off her shirt and shakes her legs to loosen the crumbs. I take the edge of the blanket in my hand and give it a shake before I roll it up to fit in the bag.

We make our way over to the playground. Ella looks at me and waits for me to tell her she can go play.

I wave her on with one hand and settle myself on the bench with the best view of the entire playground. That way I can keep an eye on her while she has fun.

I just get comfortable when I feel a weight on the other end of the bench. It is the man from earlier, the one we talked to about Ella's bracelet. I look over at him and he scoots a little closer to me.

"I think I found your granddaughter's bracelet," he says. "Is this it?"

He holds out his hand to me. In his palm lays a shiny silver bracelet with a mermaid and a seashell. He found it! Ella will be so happy. And to be honest, I am happy too.

chapter 6
Home Again

"WHAT IS YOUR NAME?" I ask the kind man who has brought back Ella's bracelet.

"I'm John."

"It is so nice to meet you, John. You've been so kind to us today," I tell him.

"Oh, it's no problem at all. I never mind helping pretty ladies," he says with a wink.

I blush like a teenager.

"Oh my," I say. I can't think of a single interesting thing to say.

"You look a little familiar to me," he says. "Did you grow up around here?"

"Yes, actually. I went to high school at Roosevelt High."

"No kidding? So did I," he replies. He takes a long look at my face, making my cheeks turn red again. I meet his nice blue eyes and wait for him to say something.

"You sat behind me in English class our senior year of high school. You had long blond hair and your name is Elizabeth." He looks at me with pride at figuring out why I look familiar.

"John Watkins?" I ask but I already know the answer. Now I can see that I do know this man from a very long time ago.

"That's me. Wow, what a small world. I haven't seen you since the summer after high school."

I shake my head yes. That is right. I am talking to someone I haven't talked to in almost fifty years.

We chat for a few minutes more about old classmates and who we keep in touch with. He tells me more about his children and grandchildren. It is a very pleasant conversation on a beautiful day.

"Where is your little girl?" he asks.

I point to Ella who is swinging as high as she can on the swings. Her feet fly up over everyone's heads and her long curls drags the ground as she leans back on the upswing.

John stands up and walks in that direction and motions for me to follow him. Ella drags her feet on the ground to slow down as we walk up to her swing.

"Look, honey. John here found your bracelet," I say to her. John holds out the bracelet by its end so she can take it from him. Her face lights up at the sight of the jewelry she thought was gone forever.

"I found it right under the bench at the dog park. I got lucky."

I hook the bracelet around Ella's wrist again and make sure it is hooked tight. She shakes it around just like the first time and listens to the charms tinkle.

I look over at John and he gives me a warm smile. He reaches out and takes my hand for a friendly handshake.

"I hope to see you around the park again, Elizabeth. We can do more catching up about the old days."

"Yes, I would like that," I say. I watch him for a moment as he walks away. I feel very happy to have met and old/new friend!

Our day at the park is almost at an end. We have explored the lake, the dog park, the playground, and even had a delicious snack in between. Ella is beginning to slow down and I think it is time we were getting back home.

We retrace our steps to get back to the giant gates at the entrance of the park. I take Ella's hand as we leave the park and set our feet on the sidewalk towards my house. She skips along beside me and I try to keep up.

My heart is happy as the perfect spring day comes to an end.

THE END

A Day At The Park – Chapter Summaries

Chapter 1 – The Call

I am comforted by the routine of setting the alarm clock, having coffee, and watching the sunrise. I'm looking for a cheerful outfit for the day....

Chapter 2 – The Gift

My morning routine includes brushing their teeth, putting on makeup, and preparing for Ella's visit to the park. Nana gives Ella a silver bracelet with three charms. We go to the park together....

Chapter 3 – Sights and Sounds

We visit a park withrolling green hills and flat ground for a picnic. Ella is ready to feed the geese and watch the turtles and fish swimming in the water...

Chapter 4 – Life Under Water

We take a long way to the lake, finding a black and gray pigeon. Ella tosses pieces of bread into the lake, attracting geese and turtles. Ella and I enjoy the sun's rays, but Ella's bracelet is missing. We plan to retrace their steps before leaving...

Chapter 5 – Lost and Found

Ella and I find a spot in the sun and shade to eat our picnice and watch the clouds float by. We listen to the sounds of a softball game. Ella goes to play in the playground. The missing bracelet is found by the kind man...

Chapter 6 – Home Again

I meet John again for the first time in almost fifty years, he is the man who found the bracelet. We chat about old classmates and their children and grandchildren. Ella and I explore some more before returning home...

THE END

SHORT STORIES

Delightful short stories
all about parks.

Short Story 1
Old Friends

MARGARET AND PAMELA slowly strolled along the park path, their arms linked and a pleasant smile on both their faces. The brightly lit park seem to invite them in, and they obliged, taking in the smell of freshly cut grass, the twitters of the birds, and the cheerful chatter of the other park goers. The two elderly ladies had been friends for decades, and as they walked through the park, they had plenty to talk about.

"Remember when we used to come here to pick flowers?" Margaret said, a smile lighting up her face as she looked around. "It must have been fifty years ago now."

Pamela nodded in agreement, her blue eyes twinkling in the sunlight. "Oh yes! I remember it like it was yesterday. We'd fill up our little baskets with the most beautiful flowers, and then head off down to the pond to have our tea parties."

Margaret chuckled softly. "Those tea parties were certainly something else. We'd always have the most outrageous spreads, and make the most interesting stories while sharing our cups of tea."

The two women smiled fondly as they reminisced about their past. As they continued walking, their conversation shifted to more recent times.

"How is your grandson doing at school?" asked Pamela, her voice soft and inquisitive.

"He's doing really well," Margaret replied. "He's in the top of his class and is always so eager to learn new things. We're all very proud of him."

Pamela smiled. "That's wonderful. You must be very proud of him."

"Yes, I certainly am," Margaret said, a note of pride in her voice.

The two continued walking, and as they did, they passed some of the park's more iconic locations. Margaret pointed out the old apple tree, where she used to pick apples for her mother's pies, and the gazebo, where she and Pamela once spent an entire afternoon chatting and laughing. Each memory was special to them, and as they recalled the past, the two friends seemed to drift back in time.

"Do you remember the summer we spent at the lake?" Margaret asked, her voice soft with nostalgia.

Pamela nodded, her smile widening. "Of course I do! We stayed up late every night talking and watching the stars. It was so peaceful and beautiful."

"It was one of the best summers of my life," Margaret said, her gaze distant and her voice full of emotion.

The two women continued down the path, arms still linked, lost in their own thoughts and memories. Before long, they found themselves in front of the park's most iconic location: the old marble fountain. The fountain was a stunning sight, with its intricate carvings and cascading water. Seeing the fountain, Margaret and Pamela paused, both lost in their own thoughts.

"It's been so long since we've been here," Pamela said quietly.

Margaret nodded in agreement. "Yes, it really has. We always used to come here when we felt like catching up."

The two ladies shared a smile, happy to be back in such a special place. With another nod, they started to slowly walk away from the fountain, both content and relaxed. As they walked, they continued to talk, discussing the past, present, and future.

"I'm so glad that we've been able to stay in touch all these years," Margaret said, her voice full of emotion.

Pamela nodded, her blue eyes twinkling. "Me too," she said, squeezing Margaret's hand.

The two friends smiled at each other and walked on, their conversation full of love and happiness. As they slowly made their way back to the park's entrance, they did not notice the other people around them, or the passing of time. All they noticed was each other, and the strong bond between them. They were two elderly friends, content to just enjoy each other's company and take in the beauty of the park around them.

As they left the park, they knew that they had many years ahead of them, and that their friendship would endure and continue to grow as the years went by. Nothing would ever be able to break the bond between them, for it was stronger than any force of nature. Margaret and Pamela had found a true friendship in each other and were content to walk through life together, hand in hand, never forgetting the special memories and moments shared all those years ago.

THE END

Short Story 2
Park Ranger

JACK ENJOYED this daily ritual; it was a reminder to him of why he had chosen to become a park ranger in the first place. As his gaze swept the meadow, he marveled at the peacefulness and beauty of it all. He could hear the birds chirping, the insects buzzing, and the faint hint of a breeze rustling the trees. The sun was low in the sky and its orange light shone through the clouds like a halo, making the whole scene even more magical.

Jack continued his stroll, taking it all in as he walked along the quiet path. He stopped to admire the blooming wildflowers that lined the edge of the meadow, their petals unfurling in the cool breeze. He saw the pond, glimmering in the fading light, its still surface reflecting the deep blue sky. He paused then to watch a family of ducks quacking and paddling their way through the water.

As he continued his journey, Jack started noticing the small creatures that inhabit the park: rabbits and squirrels darting across the grass; birds perched in the trees, singing their songs; and butterflies flitting through the air, their wings a bright and vibrant blur of color. Everywhere he looked, he could see signs of life, each and every one of them unique and special in its own way.

Jack knew that the beauty of Central Park wasn't just what could be seen on the surface. There was much more beneath, hidden away in the shadows of the trees and the tall buildings that surround it. It was a living, breathing organism, where humans and animals had coexisted for centuries. He felt a deep connection to this place, and was reminded of how important it was to protect it.

As Jack continued his stroll, he noticed something else: a group of people gathered around the edge of the meadow, chatting and laughing. He realized that it was a group of school kids, who were talking about the wildlife and pointing excitedly at the animals that were just out of reach.

Jack spent the rest of his day at Central Park in full ranger mode, helping visitors of all ages to discover and explore its natural wonders. He led guided nature walks and taught classes about local flora and fauna, giving children and adults alike the chance to learn more about their environment.

He also answered questions from those curious about the park's history, pointing out key landmarks or pointing out interesting facts about certain species of birds that could be heard but not seen.

At the end of the day, Jack felt a sense of accomplishment and satisfaction knowing that he had helped others appreciate and understand their surroundings a bit better. As he walked back to the ranger station, he was filled with a newfound respect for this urban wilderness - and an even greater desire to protect it.

THE END

Short Story 3
Model Boats

Michael steadied the model boat as his grandson Andy leaned in and tried to adjust the sail. The little craft rocked in the breeze as Andy fumbled with the lines.

"It's alright," Michael said. "Take your time. That's how you learn."

Andy smiled, feeling the warmth of his grandfather's encouraging words. "I'm trying," he said.

Michael nodded. He knew that Andy had been eager to learn how to sail a model boat since he had first noticed them at the park. It was a skill that had been passed down through the generations of Michael's family, a legacy that he was proud to share.

The schooner-style model boat was a thing of beauty with its tall, triangular mainsail and mast of varnished wood. The white hull glistened in the sun, while the mast stood proudly above the water.

Michael smiled. "She's a beauty, isn't she? I built her from scratch, when I was about your age. Now let's see if we can get her moving."

Michael reached out to adjust the sail himself, but quickly stopped when he saw the disappointment in Andy's expression. With a few more words of encouragement, Michael stepped back and watched as Andy slowly began to get the hang of it.

The sun was beating down, but the breeze coming off the pond kept them cool. The grass in the park was lush and green, and the trees swayed gently in the wind. Michael watched as Andy maneuvered the boat in the water, making sure to keep an eye on the wind direction so he could adjust the sails.

Michael smiled at the sight, proud of his grandson. The two generations of sailors, generations apart in age but just as passionate about the craft, were connected in the moment.

As the sun began to set and the shadows grew longer, Michael and Andy gathered up the model boat and headed back to the park entrance. Andy was smiling the whole way, still marveling at his new skills.

Just before they left, Michael stopped and looked back at the pond. In the fading light, he could just make out the silhouette of the little boat that Andy had been sailing — a reminder of the bond that the two of them had formed.

Michael touched Andy's shoulder and said softly, "I want you to know that this is something we can always do together."

Andy smiled and nodded, taking his grandfather's words to heart. He knew that this was only the beginning of something great.

THE END

Short Story 4
Checkmate

IT WAS a beautiful Sunday morning in the park, the sun beaming down on the lush green grass, the leaves of the trees rustling in the wind. Carl and John were two old friends, meeting up in the park almost every Sunday morning to play a game of chess. They had been doing this for more than thirty years, but recently other commitments had prevented them.

The two men greeted each other warmly, shaking hands, then sat down on the wooden benches that flanked the chessboard.

"It's been too long," Carl said. "I've missed our games."

John smiled and nodded. "It has been a while. How have you been?"

Carl shrugged. "I've been alright. I just feel like something's missing."

John nodded. "It feels like time is passing us by so quickly. We don't have much control over it. The only thing we can control is how we make use of our time."

Carl looked at the chessboard and sighed. "Yes, I suppose you're right. We should make the most of it."

John leaned back in his chair and looked out over the park. "It's beautiful, isn't it? I feel so lucky to have this place to come to."

Carl smiled. "It's amazing how much our lives can change in just a few years, yet this park has been here for over a century. It's like a timeless reminder of how the simple things in life matter most."

John nodded. "It is a reminder of what's truly important."

The two friends looked at the board, considering the possibilities. Carl moved first, making a careful move that would set up his defense. John responded with a surprisingly aggressive move. The game was on.

The two men talked strategy and shared stories as they played. It was clear that this was more than just a game of chess for them; it was a reminder of days gone by. They talked about their families, their work, and their lives in general.

As the game progressed, Carl and John began to recall the adventures they had shared in the past. They laughed and reminisced about the good times and the bad. Despite the passing of the years, the bond that they shared was still strong.

Finally, Carl checkmated John. The two men shook hands and smiled.

"Well done," John said. "That was quite a game."

Carl smiled. "Yes, it was. I'm glad that we're still able to enjoy this every Sunday."

John nodded. "It's a reminder that the simple things in life matter most. We should cherish them and not take them for granted."

The two men packed up their chess set and said their goodbyes. As Carl walked away, he smiled and thought about how lucky he was to have such a wonderful friend. Timeless memories, indeed.

THE END

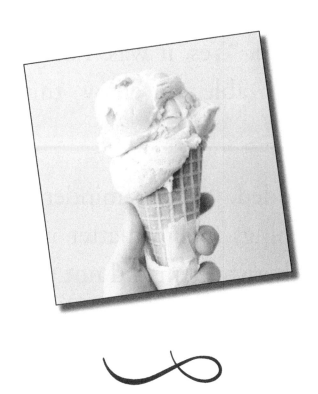

Short Story 5
Ice Cream

HENRY had been sitting in the park beneath the tall willow tree for what felt like an eternity, his silver ice cream cart parked just in front of him, the gleaming metal glinting in the sun.

He had brought a variety of flavors and toppings with him: chocolate, strawberry, vanilla and blueberry, as well as sprinkles, gummy bears, chocolate chips, and coconut flakes. Everyone in the park could smell the sweet aroma of his wares, and Henry could almost feel their mouths watering in anticipation.

There was a soft breeze blowing through the park that day, rustling the leaves in the trees, and for a moment, Henry was almost lulled into a peaceful state. But then he heard a sound – the sound of children's laughter. He was jolted back to reality and looked up to see a group of children running towards him.

The children were ecstatic as they rushed to get their ice creams, their conversations and laughter bubbling up with excitement. They arrived at the cart and Henry beamed at them, relieved to finally have some customers. The children began to debate amongst themselves about what flavors to get, and he took it as a personal challenge to have them all happy with their choices.

"Ah, for you I have something special," he said, reaching for the sprinkles. He added them to cones filled with different flavors: the blueberry for the little girl with the bright yellow dress, the strawberry for the boy with the mop of brown hair, and the chocolate for the boy with the gap-toothed smile. He placed the gummy bears onto the cones of the two little ones, and they squealed with delight.

The children stood around the cart, happily licking their ice creams and conversing with one another.

Henry looked around the park and saw many other children and adults, now heading his way. He was suddenly overwhelmed with joy—he had made it, and now the park was filled with people wanting his sweet treats.

He began to dole out the cones and cups of ice cream to the crowd, offering different flavors and combinations to suit each customer's individual tastes. Henry watched in delight as the children licked their ice creams, their faces illuminated with joy, and the adults contentedly licking and savoring their treats.

He was happy to see everyone in the park so happy, and he continued to hand out the ice creams until all of his supplies had run out.

Finally, Henry looked up and saw the park was now empty and it was time for him to go home. He beamed with pride and satisfaction—his ice cream cart had brought happiness to all of his customers, and he had done a good job. That was the best feeling of all.

THE END

Short Story 6
Richmond Park

JOE STOOD looking out across Richmond Park in England. From his vantage point atop a small hill, he could see the entire expanse of the park in the early morning light. Rolling meadows and tall trees stretched out as far as the eye could see.

It was still that peaceful hour before the day was fully awake, when the birds were just beginning to stir and the soft morning breeze brought the scent of wildflowers to his nose.

Joe smiled to himself, feeling the peace of the moment. He loved this part of his job, the early morning hours before the bustle of the day began.

Every day he would come to Richmond Park to work, and every morning he would be the first one there. It was his own little slice of heaven.

Joe turned his attention to the tasks at hand. He looked out across the grass, spied his shovel and wheelbarrow standing by the small pile of topsoil, and began to plan his day.

He would start with the flower beds he had been assigned to plant. They were one of the many projects he was charged with, but this was one of his favourites.

Joe loved to plant, to take the bare soil and turn it into a place of beauty. He had a special talent for it, and it showed in the delicate blooms he coaxed out of the ground.

He grabbed his shovel and wheelbarrow, and headed to the flower beds. As he walked, he noticed the dew still sparkling on the grass and the first rays of the rising sun glinting off the leaves of the trees. He took a deep breath of the morning air, feeling energized and ready to begin his work.

At the flower beds, he surveyed his work. He had been assigned to plant a variety of flowers that would add colour and beauty to the park.

He got to work, carefully digging a hole in the centre of each bed and then filling it with soil. Once each hole was filled, he used his shovel to smooth out the surface and then planted the flowers in their designated spots.

Joe took extra care to ensure each one was planted with the right depth and an even spacing between the plants.

As he worked, his mind drifted back to his childhood. He remembered the days when he used to come to Richmond Park with his family, how he would run and play among the trees and flowers, always with a sense of wonder.

Joesmiled, thinking of how much he had enjoyed those days. His love of gardening had grown from that time, and now he found himself here, planting these beautiful blooms.

After placing the last of the flowers in the beds, Joe paused to take a look around. Everything was in its place, and the beds were ready to be adorned with the colourful blooms of the upcoming season.

He stood there for a few moments, listening to the birds singing in the trees and feeling the warmth of the morning sun on his face, and he was filled with a deep sense of satisfaction. He had done good work today, and soon the park would be alive with the vivid colours of the flowers he had planted.

He took one last look around, and with a smile on his face, he picked up his shovel and wheelbarrow, and began the journey back to his shed. He may not have been able to stay and witness the beauty he had created, but he knew that soon enough, the flowers he had planted would be a testament to the hard work and dedication he had put into the job.

As the light of the day grew, Joe walked back to his shed with a sense of pride and contentment. He knew the flowers were going to bring joy to many. And as he reached his shed, he looked up and saw a single ray of sunshine peeking through the clouds, giving him a glimpse of the future beauty of Richmond Park.

THE END

Short Story 7
Childhood Memories

CHARLES AND EMMA arrived at the park, full of energy and anticipation. The air was crisp and the sky a bright blue, laced with wisps of white clouds.

As they approached the entrance, they pushed and prodded each other playfully, anxious to get to the fun.

Once they were in, they took in the sights. The swings hung motionless, waiting to take flight with joyous riders. The see-saw stood ready, begging to be pushed up and down. The slide was a tall, gleaming metal structure, beckoning with its promise of a swift descent. Finally, there was the roundabout, an old-fashioned carousel with painted horses and a central pole rising high into the sky.

Charles and Emma decided to start with the swings. Charles held the chain firmly as Emma jumped in, squealing with delight. He pushed her gently, just enough to get her going. She laughed and held onto the chains tighter as the swing rose higher and higher.

They continued to take turns, with Charles pushing Emma higher and higher and Emma squealing with delight. Charles let himself get lost in his memories of when he was a child. He remembered the feeling of the sun on his face, the wind in his hair, and the sensation of his stomach rising and falling as the swing moved higher and higher.

Charles laughed and Emma joined in, her face bright and shining.

When they were both done with the swings, they moved on to the see-saw. Charles sat down on one side and Emma on the other. She giggled as Charles pushed her up and down, their weight balancing out, up and down, up and down. Charles marveled at the sensation of it, the memory of it as sharp and clear as the day he had first experienced it.

From the see-saw, they moved to the slide. Here, Emma took the lead, going up and down the winding metal structure, laughing and screeching with glee. Charles followed behind, admiring her enthusiasm and joy.

Lastly, they went to the roundabout. Charles took Emma's hand and they stepped onto the moving platform. As it began to move, Emma grabbed tightly onto the pole. Charles jumped onto the back of a horse, planting his feet firmly on its mane.

The roundabout slowly spun, taking them on a journey back in time. Charles closed his eyes, and the memories of his childhood flooded back to him. He saw himself flying high with the wind in his face and the sun on his skin. He remembered the carefree feeling of happiness and freedom he used to have when riding the roundabout.

When the ride stopped, Charles and Emma stepped off and walked back to the entrance hand in hand. They had spent the entire afternoon together, laughing and playing in the park. Charles could see the joy and the sense of accomplishment in Emma's face.

He knew that he had given her a glimpse of his childhood, and that she had enjoyed every second of it. For Charles, riding the swings, see-saw, slide, and roundabout had been like traveling back in time. He had experienced a little piece of his childhood once again, and it had been wonderful.

As they left the park, both feeling content and exhausted, Charles silently thanked the heavens for the day he had shared with his granddaughter. He had been able to give her a little bit of his past, and for that he was truly thankful.

THE END

Short Story 8
Flowers

SHE HAD been told it was a lovely park, but as she stepped onto the winding path, with tall trees casting their shadows over the path, she was overwhelmed with a sense of peace and calm. She felt like she was in a different world, a world where time stopped and all the worries of her life stopped.

The path was lined by perfectly manicured flower beds, and she couldn't help but stop to admire the beauty of each one. She noticed the delicate pink petals of anemones, the lush green of hydrangeas, and the bright yellow of daffodils. She was captivated by the variety of colors and shapes of the flowers, so much so that she almost forgot why she was there.

But then she remembered the roses. She had been told that this park was famous for its roses, so she had made her way here with the intention of finding some. Sure enough, there were dozens of them lining the path, in various shades of pink and red.

The scent of the roses is sweet and inviting, like a bouquet of fresh-cut flowers, with hints of citrus and honey.

She had never seen such beautiful roses before, and as she walked by them, she couldn't help but reach out to touch their velvety petals.

Each petal was perfect in its own way, with delicate edges that seemed to glow in the light.

As she moved further along the path, she noticed the flutter of butterflies, and she couldn't help but smile. She watched as they flitted from one flower to the next, and she stopped to admire their brilliant colors and delicate wings. She was struck by their beauty, and the sight made her heart swell with joy.

At the end of the path, she reached a small pond. The water was so still that she could see her reflection in it. She was struck by the beauty of the scene, and she was filled with a sense of awe and appreciation. She knew that she would always remember this moment.

As she continued her journey through the park, she paused frequently to admire the beauty of the roses. She noticed that some of them were tangled together, creating the most beautiful bouquet of colors. Other roses seemed like they were dancing in the wind, their petals swaying in the breeze.

She also marveled at how the sunlight danced across the petals of the roses, and how the dewdrops sparkled like diamonds in the morning light. She was entranced by the beauty of the park, and as she looked around, she realized that she had never seen such an enchanting place.

The birds were singing softly in the trees, and the scent of the flowers filled the air. She was overwhelmed with a feeling of contentment and joy, and she knew that she had found a place of relaxation and wonder. She was so glad that she had decided to take a walk through the park.

THE END

THANK YOU

Visit **seniorality.com** for access to a wide range of books, stories, word searches, coloring pages, audio book videos, a monthly magazine, and more.

A Day At The Park -
Jamie Stonebridge, Misty Gardner

Old Friends, Park Ranger
Model Boats, Checkmate
Ice Cream, Richmond Park
Childhood Memories, Flowers -
Sam Suncroft

Set in 22 pt EB Garamond

seniorality.com
Quality Time for Seniors

LAUNCHING IN SEPTEMBER 2023

ORDER YOUR MAGAZINE NOW
seniorality.com

Printed in Great Britain
by Amazon

38818306R00067